Great Presentations

Great Presentations

✦

How to Keep Your Audiences Awake - All the Time

Leonard Sklar, author of "The Check Is NOT In The Mail"

GREAT PRESENTATIONS
HOW TO KEEP YOUR AUDIENCES AWAKE - ALL THE TIME

iUniverse books may be ordered through booksellers or by contacting:

iUniverse
1663 Liberty Drive
Bloomington, IN 47403
www.iuniverse.com
844-349-9409

ISBN: 978-0-5954-7149-2 (sc)
ISBN: 978-0-5959-1430-2 (e)

Print information available on the last page.

iUniverse rev. date: 08/06/2020

Contents

1

WHY THIS BOOK?

Seminars, workshops, and presentations (I use the terms interchangeably) serve basically to educate or sell a product, service or idea, at a level beyond a one-on-one interchange. Venues that may benefit include, for example, classrooms, military briefings, religious gatherings, and internal organization communication efforts, as well as the traditional sales and promotional gatherings.

The material covered in a seminar may be quite basic, highly technical, deeply psychological or all of the above. In many such seminar programs, individual audience members may experience resistance to change, difficulty or reluctance to learn new material, serious disagreement with what is presented, and any combination of these, including those "participants" who were forced to attend and really don't want to be there, or those folks who are just happy to have an excuse to get out of work that day.

Bearing these realities in mind, and in consideration of the goals of the seminar producer to accomplish something positive as a result of the effort expended, my purpose in writing this book is to point out as many of the ways that I have learned, in over 30 years of conducting seminars, by which those goals are *not* achieved and why that happens, as well as the positive methods for producing consistently outstanding programs.

Putting it even more positively, I want to share with you how you *can* improve the odds that more of the audience will gain, from the experience, more of the goals you intend for them to get. Note that I will use the term "experience" often. The reason is that the communications in a seminar impact both the "right brain" as well as the "left brain", no matter how technical the material. More on these terms, and their importance, in chapter nine.

The point is that there will be, inevitably, degrees of resistance to learning or "getting" the message that the seminar leader wants to convey. To the degree that the leader can maximize the number of participants who fully learn or "get" what is intended, the seminar will achieve its goals. This objective is, however, extraordinarily difficult to achieve.

Many seminar presenters are not aware of the levels and forms of resistance or that expected goals are falling far short of being achieved. Those of us who have been to a seminar that left us shaking our heads in disappointment or fell asleep for a while, know how difficult it is to produce a truly powerful seminar experience.

Learning to cope more effectively with the many forms of resistance to learning would also be of direct value for teachers in their classrooms, as I will describe further in chapter nine, resulting, hopefully, in a better educated citizenry.

Part of what contributes to a successful seminar is the presentation and interaction with the audience. Part is the physical environment of the room, the marketing or arrangements made for the audience to be there, and part is the followup, whenever that is possible and appropriate.

So, we have a lot of work to do and details to master before achieving the ideal seminar. You can also expect that it will take time—often a year or more—to get to the highest levels of achievement. The ultimate goal for any seminar presenter is what I call "serving the audience". During the course of reading this book, you will discover more of what that phrase means and how crucial it is, because *everything* the seminar presenter does *must* have that as its purpose.

I have organized the book into the following chapters:

Now, read on to learn, or review, how to become a master in producing and presenting a first-rate seminar, every time.

2

THE TYPICAL BAD SEMINAR

There are so many ways that a seminar will *not* achieve some or most of its objectives. Here, in random order, are many of the ways to fall short. This list by no means covers every possible way of short changing the audience. It does, however, provide a source for the kinds of things to avoid as you become ever more proficient in being the best seminar presenter you can be.

- Talk in a monotone or inaudibly, too loud, or with poor English.
- Have the room be too hot or too cold.
- Make inappropriate jokes.
- Pace around the front of the room.
- Keep looking at your watch.
- Do not invite questions.
- Rush through your material.
- Rely too heavily on visual material.
- Do not invite an evaluation of the seminar by each attendee.
- Endure audience reading handouts while you are speaking.
- Let a few individuals "hog" the questions.
- Dress inappropriately.
- Push your product or service too aggressively, or not at all.
- Don't bother getting attendance credits for attendees, when they are of value to them.

- Eat something during your presentation.
- Jingle change in your pocket.
- Hold back the "really good material" to encourage them to buy it from you afterward.
- Use curse words.
- Don't bother asking if the audience understands or "gets" what you said.
- Ignore the loud noise coming from the room next door.
- Start 20 minutes late.
- Don't be available during breaks to answer questions.
- Don't bother making sure the room is set up correctly.
- Make fun of an audience member's question or comment.
- Go a half hour over the ending time.
- Try to act like someone else you admire.

As I said, this is not meant to be a complete list, but I think you will get the idea. The list is really intended to give you an incentive to read *all* the chapters of the book, since the more of these no-no's you do, the less effective will be your results.

3

MY BACKGROUND

At this point, I should describe my background and experience for advising others on how to produce the best possible seminars.

The bottom line is: I have created and successfully presented literally thousands of seminars. Here's a brief history that led to this outcome.

I began my business career after graduating from Franklin & Marshall College in 1956. The next 14 years were spent as an industrial engineer at Procter & Gamble, an economist at Dow Chemical, and a salesman for IBM's Service Bureau Corporation.

I eventually felt the need to start and manage my own company. After looking around for a while, I settled on a collection agency because it didn't take that much money to start one, and the poor reputation of many of them suggested to me that, with my business experience, I could make a go of it.

I began in January, 1970, knowing very little about the business, but I was successful in selling the service and, within a year, I knew what the business was all about. I learned that businesses tend to sit on unpaid accounts far too long before calling in the pros, they make too few, too clumsy, or just no collection phone calls, they have poor or no payment policies, and they are really reluctant to ask for the money due them.

These insights led me to a breakthrough idea; namely, to teach businesses how to *avoid* collection problems, in the first place and then how to recover as much as possible themselves, more quickly, at less cost, and without losing valued customers, so that they could minimize how many accounts they had to turn over to collection agencies like mine. I even invited my own clients to attend. Many of my competitors thought it was madness to give away all of our secrets, but I learned that the more I told the audience, the more they realized what amateurs they were compared to the pros, so I got accounts from my clients more quickly, which made them more collectable, I got referrals from them, and I gained many new clients grateful for such useful information.

My first seminar was 30 minutes long, and I read the whole thing, word for word, with my knuckles turning white from clutching the podium too tightly. Eventually, I got better at it, continuing with two hour seminars, then four hour, and eventually six hours.

I grew the seminar business to the point that I was producing 600 seminars a year, in 200 U. S. cities in all 50 states, and I trained 12 other people to be presenters. This went on for 20 years. We had the reputation of being the best in the business. We knew this because we had each seminar attendee fill out a detailed evaluation form after every seminar, which is one way I knew how each of my other seminar leaders was doing. And, in many cities, people from the same organization returned again and again, because after they put into effect what they considered were the easier insights gained from an earlier seminar, they were ready and eager to listen to, and profit from, some of the same information that they had resisted previously.

My company mailed 2 ½ million brochures a year, and our audiences averaged 40 to 60 people, although we would do a seminar for as few as 10 people, occasionally, and we frequently worked with over 150, as many as 600 one time.

I produced several collection audio and video programs, other collection training tools and wrote an industry standard book, "The Check Is

NOT In The Mail". All products were sold at the seminar and were pictured on the promotional brochure, so that people could buy them, whether or not they attended the seminar. I did a lot of consulting and training, and I still do an occasional seminar upon request. I was a guest on CNBC, FNN, ABC, and several radio programs.

I also created one of the first collection temp staffing companies and grew that to twelve offices nationwide.

Since collecting and selling have many common characteristics, I conducted many very powerful selling seminars and trainings that featured advanced role playing. You can read about these in chapter eight, where you'll also learn what are the common elements of these two important business disciplines.

From all of this experience, I believe I am well qualified to help others become the best they can be in producing and presenting a powerful seminar. I intend to leave nothing out.

4

LOGISTICS

Although the content and presentation of a seminar may appear more important than the environment in which it is presented, those environmental, or logistical, elements are crucial to a totally successful event. Put another way, without the right logistics, the overall experience can range from merely adequate to truly miserable. A simple example is a room that is too cold, which tends to focus the mind on that assault to the body rather than on the material being presented. Here, then, are key logistical issues you need to handle correctly.

- **Initial Room Arrangements**—When you contact the place where the meeting will be held, let them know that you will give a final count of attendees two to three days in advance, along with a diagram of the room setup, the coffee order, and other details described below. Find out how many people the room will hold if it is set up classroom-style—chairs with table in front—or theater style—chairs with no tables.

  Avoid rooms with columns, if possible, and avoid rooms that are long and narrow. The best shape is square or rectangular (but not a long, narrow rectangle). Check to be sure that the lighting in the room will allow people to see anything you write on a flipchart or read information in the material you hand out.

  If you are providing lunch, whether included in the program cost or participant-paid, ask the facility to reserve a separate room or area of the lunchroom for your people. Then, when lunchtime arrives, tell your audience to let the lunchroom staff know that they are the people for whom the area has been set aside. This process allows the lunch period to go as planned, time-wise. Otherwise, people will be late returning after the lunch period ends, and they will either miss the material you start the afternoon with or you will delay the start time.

Then, two to three days in advance, fax or e-mail a diagram of how you want the room set up along with your coffee order, whether or not you want a platform in front, what's on the front of the room area, such as a podium and flipchart.

Above all, ask that the room be set up the night before. If that's not possible, you want the setup crew to do the job early in the morning, because, in either case, you will need to check that the setup is as you requested and, in my experience, you will make some adjustments in the physical layout. Even better is to be at the room while it's being set up, so that you can direct the crew to make any necessary adjustments in aisle width, table placement, etc., so that you don't have to do those by yourself.

- **<u>Room Setup On Seminar Day</u>**—Here are the key components:

  1. If there is enough room, it is ideal to set up the room all classroom style, which gives attendees a place to put their water or coffee and makes for easier note taking. With a smaller room or if the attendance is greater than expected, a combination of classroom style in the front of the room followed by just chairs (theater style) behind, works just fine.

  2. Always add seats for 10% more people than you expect. The reason is that you don't want the last two or three people looking for the last two or three seats, which will be hard to find and is disruptive. For this reason, also have extra chairs stacked up in the back for last minute, unexpected, participants.

  3. If the room has windows and blinds, pull the blinds so that you eliminate the distraction of people looking outside instead of concentrating on what you are covering. If the walls of the room are thin and you can expect to hear the people next door,

go to the presenter next door, before your seminar begins, and tell them that if they will keep the volume level down, you will too. That usually produces cooperation. Naturally, when ordering the room, in the first place, ask if the room has thin, usually moveable, walls, and avoid that room.

4.   The arrangement of seats is important. Have the first row begin approx. three feet from the front of your speaking area, if there is no raised podium, or four feet, if there is a podium. The reason is that you don't want to tower over the people in the front row, which has them craning their necks looking up at you.

5.   Most folding tables will seat three people comfortably. If there are three or more tables on either side of an aisle, swing the end tables of the first row or rows forward, at an angle, so as to face the speaker, or those people will be uncomfortably turning their heads throughout the seminar.

6.   Adjust the rows of seats so that the back of the chairs in each row, when people are sitting in them, are approx. 18 inches from the front of the seats in the row behind. This is so that people can get in and out of their seats comfortably.

7.   For the average speaker, no mike is needed for up to 50 or 60 people. Above that number, a mike can be useful.

8.   Have cold water, hot water and tea bags, and coffee available. Decaf coffee will usually satisfy those used to regular, but you can have both, if you wish. A gallon of coffee usually produces 20 cups, but since everyone does not drink coffee and some will have more than one cup, a formula I have found useful most of the time is to order on the basis of 25 cups to a gallon. In other words, for 75 people, you order three gallons. Occasionally, you will have to add more, and you do so by ordering by the carafe, not by the gallon.

9.   Try to get a room in which the temperature can be controlled with a thermometer in the room. Set it initially at 70 degrees.

I'll discuss later how and when to change it to meet the needs of the majority of the audience. Incidentally, there is a notion that many people hold that when a lot of people enter a room, the temperature will go up dramatically. Not so—it will go up only slightly.

10. It usually is helpful to provide each attendee with a pen or pencil, plus a notepad. Hotels usually have these available at no cost.

11. If you have products to sell later, have them laid out on a table in back of the room, as you are setting it up. You will talk about them during or at the end of the program.

12. If you have a registration table outside the room, you may want to provide nametags, which are helpful for both the seminar presenter—to call on or acknowledge people by name—as well as for the participants, who may want to chat with each other, as is common.

5

BASIC SEMINAR CONCEPTS

In this chapter, I will describe several key points of view to always keep in mind when presenting a seminar. Many of these points will require further discussion in later chapters. The following concepts and specifics are designed to create a mind-set that you take with you for any presentation you will make.

1. Your overall objective is to "serve the audience". This will take a while to become clear, as I've stated earlier, but, for now, the idea is to answer every aspect of what you do in a seminar by asking, "Will this serve the audience?"

2. You are the expert, but you don't have to think that you need to know everything. If you don't know the answer to a question, you can say so, ask the audience if any one knows the answer, or you can say that you will find out and get back to them.

3. Do not provide personal distractions. Specifically, dress appropriately, do not pace around the front of the room, do take off your watch at the beginning of the program and place it on the podium, where you can look at it unobtrusively, keep your hands out of your pockets, and avoid excessive gestures. It is OK to sip water or coffee from time to time.

4. Don't be preachy, smug, or act like a know-it-all.

5. Lecturing can be a relatively poor way of communicating. Make it a point of getting feedback, even with a PowerPoint or slide presentation.

6. The corollary is to get as much interaction as possible.

7. The audience for a public seminar will usually vary a lot. Early in the seminar, ask, with a show of hands, for levels of experience, positions in the organization, etc. This approach helps bring some audience members together, and it allows you to better gauge what kind of audience you are working with. Look for more on this point in the next chapter, item #7.

8. Avoid the temptation to rush ahead just to be sure you cover all the material you planned to discuss. It's far better to cover well what you can in the time available and to let your audience know that that is what you are doing.

9. Do not succumb to the temptation to hold back sharing your most valuable information, on the grounds that your services will not be needed afterward. The opposite is true. Sharing your expertise makes it clear that the audience members are amateurs compared to you. Bear in mind that your "best stuff" took a long time to acquire and really understand, and others will not pick it up in an instant or even in a few hours.

10. Some people in the audience will resist what you are saying, whether spoken aloud or not, and some will openly disagree with you. Welcome and encourage these honest statements of where people's thoughts and feelings are at, so that you can deal with them. Specific ways of doing this are discussed in chapter nine.

11. Have fun whenever appropriate. Even difficult or highly technical subjects can be absorbed more easily if you can lighten up, and a good laugh or chuckle can help people stay conscious and become closer to one another.

12. The single most important attitude you must acquire is to get out of your head and into those of your audience. In other words, stop worrying about how you are doing, and place your attention on how the audience is doing. Specific ways of doing this are covered in detail in chapters eight and nine.

6

CONDUCTING THE PROGRAM

How you start the program says a lot about how your audience perceives you and your ability to accomplish your goals. Handling all of the following pointers successfully establishes you as a pro; that is, someone to pay attention to.

1. Whatever the starting time, expect some people to be late. The problem with delaying is that there will be people in the audience who took the trouble to be on time, and some of them will resent delays just because other people can't be as punctual as they are.

    On the other hand, due to heavy traffic, for example, some late-comers couldn't help being late and may resent your not accommodating them a little. My solution is to make a brief announcement at the official starting time that a few people got held up, so we will give them a few more minutes, and then we will get going. I usually wait five minutes and then start the program. I also tell the latecomers that they really haven't missed anything important.

    I recently attended a seminar that was advertised to start at 12:30. As the clock approached 12:45, some people got up and left, obviously irritated at the unacknowledged delay. The seminar presenter explained, "Oh, 12:30 is just the seating time. We don't start until12:45". Obviously, everyone, including those who left, would have liked to know that.

15

2. Another thoughtful gesture for the last few people who come into the room, either before the program starts as well as after, is to let them know where the open seats are. In some instances, I will ask people who are spread out at a table or in a row to move together to allow a group of two or three people to sit together.

3. One more observation about seating: early arrivers often sit in the back of the room. I usually make a light-hearted comment about the best seats being in front, or that I usually call on the people in the back first, which usually gets most of them moving up.

4. If you are to be introduced by someone, you should write out what you would like them to say, which will be your background relevant to today's presentation. The introducer can always add personal comments to this.

5. Your introductory comments should include a question about room temperature, because there's nothing more continuously annoying than a room that's too hot or too cold. The general "script" goes as follows, "I want to do a temperature check, because some people may be too hot or too cold, and we need to make the room as comfortable as possible for the majority of the people here today. So, by a show of hands, how many are too cold right now (wait for the response), too warm right now (wait again), and how many feel the temperature is pretty much OK as it is?" Then, adjust the temperature or leave it alone, depending on the vote and how you interpret it. Also, tell your audience that you will check with them during the program to see if the temperature is still OK (it does change) and be sure to do that about every hour or so. I often have volunteered to loan my jacket to someone, usually a woman, who is cold. Incidentally, the first time I ask for a show of hands, I include, for fun, the question, "And let's have a show of hands for those of you who don't like to raise your hands."

6. Tell your audience how you will handle questions. I'll describe later how I handle this, but you want to be sure you say how YOU will handle this key issue.

7. For many types of seminars, ask the audience what they would like to accomplish today. If you have a large flip chart on an easel, write the shorthand versions of what is said. This process accomplishes several important objectives:

    a. It allows some people to see that they are not alone in what they feel a need for.

    b. It helps get people participating right away.

    c. It opens up the shy ones if you ask, occasionally, regarding a topic someone has mentioned, "Who else here wants to get this today?"

    d. If the audience fails to mention a topic that you know should be included, based on your experience, *you* mention that topic and ask, with a show of hands, who wants to know more about it.

8. Another good device for helping both you and audience members to become more comfortable with each other is to ask, by a show of hands, where are the bosses and who are staff, who knows the topic of the seminar fairly well and who doesn't, then ask for years of experience in the subject, starting with a year or more, five, 10, 15, 20, and more than 20. Tell the most senior people, jokingly, that if you get into trouble, you'll come to them for answers. I often do go to these old pros, if only to have them confirm and reinforce what I have just said.

9. Announce what you will be covering today, when the breaks and lunch (if any) will be taken and how long they will be, and confirm when you will end.

10. Describe your background in enough detail to establish you as qualified to be in front of the room.

11. If there are handouts, I like ask the audience to go through them with me, quickly, flipping through the pages and with me describing, in a few word, what's covered. I then tell them that we will discuss these points in detail when we come to that part of the seminar. In this way, I minimize the likelihood of most of the participants flipping through the workbook while I am speaking or questions are being handled.

12. If you have a product or a service to offer, let them know how and when you will discuss that. If you will ask for an evaluation at the end, let them know that, also. Describe the purpose of the evaluation as a way to help make your program as good as it can be, just as others previously took the trouble to make *this* seminar the best it could be.

For many, or even most, people, it's normal to be a bit nervous the first few times they get in front of an audience. Frankly, most people would rather have a root canal done than speak in front of a group. So, I'm going to tell you a true story that illustrates how and how not to handle this common problem.

In the early days of my presenting seminars, since I always worked with a local company that I would refer business to, I had the manager of that company make a brief presentation on a subject that he or she was an expert on, so that the audience would have added reasons to be comfortable about considering their service. It was in Fresno, CA where I asked the manager, before the seminar began, how he felt about speaking, and he admitted that he was pretty nervous.

I asked him if he would like to hear a suggestion about how to handle that. He agreed eagerly. I told him to say something like this to the audience as he began, "Folks, if it looks as though I'm nervous, I am. My hands are shaking, my mouth is dry, and my socks are soaked." I told him that this would not only help him get through his nervousness and actually be speaking, but the majority of the audience would be able to relate to him if they were in a similar situation.

He disagreed. He said, "No, I can talk myself out of this", and off he went. So, I began the seminar, and when it was his turn to speak, he started out with, "Folks, if it looks as though I'm nervous, I am………..". It was the exact script I gave him that he rejected earlier. So, at the next break, I asked him what happened to change his mind.

He told me that he had every intention of talking himself out of his nervousness, so he went through the halls of the hotel, saying to himself, "I will not be nervous, I will not be nervous, I *will not* be nervous, and then I walked right into the ladies restroom. That's when I realized I better try it your way."

I eventually learned to avoid using any outside speakers, unless I knew they were professionals, because the amateur can easily "lose" the audience, and it takes too much time to get them back, which hurts the overall impact of the seminar.

7

HANDLING QUESTIONS

How you handle questions can make or break your program. Even if you make an all-Powerpoint or other visual presentation, you should take questions at the end, at least. There are opportunities as well as pitfalls in how you handle questions. The most basic benefit is that how well you deal with questions can allow you to better gauge how well individual audience members are with you, or not, on what you are trying to convey. Here, then, are the key considerations about questions you need to master in order to be the best you can be.

1. Encourage questions. Explain that one person's question may well be on the mind of others who haven't spoken.

2. Let the audience know that you will either answer the question if you have a pertinent response, ask if anyone in the audience knows the answer, in case *you* don't, or you will make every effort to get back to them afterward.

3. Some questions can be answered directly. Others may require role playing, which is discussed in detail in the next chapter. An example of a question that should be role played is, "What should I say if....". That type of question usually results in a back and forth dialogue, not just an answer.

4. Suppose someone has several questions. Tell them you will take one, maybe two, but then you will let some other people ask questions and, time permitting, get back to this person.

5. This brings me to the "question hog". You want to acknowledge them by congratulating them for asking questions that others may

have but are too shy to ask, but you will also control how many you take at one time. Incidentally, you are at all times in control of the seminar, although you do it in a benevolent, unobtrusive manner. It is not uncommon for someone to act as though the seminar was all about them and their questions or issues. With these people, offer to talk with them at the break or at the end of the program.

6. If someone makes a flat-out false statement, feel free to openly disagree with them and, if you feel the need to, ask if anyone else sees it the way you do.

7. Suppose someone makes a statement instead of asking a question. You may want to ask if there is a question about that or you can just thank them for the statement.

8. REPEAT QUESTIONS! You can paraphrase, if necessary.

9. Some people ramble. They go on and on, often repeating themselves and don't know how to stop. You need to handle these people gently but firmly, because the audience tends to become annoyed at the waste of time. There are two proven ways to deal with the rambler.

   a. Interrupt part way through the ramble, when it becomes repetitive, by saying, "Excuse me. Let me see if I understand what you have said so far." Then paraphrase and ask, "Is that pretty much it?" or words to that effect. Then, answer the question or respond to the comment, if there is no question.

   b. Interrupt part way through, as before, and say, "Excuse me, but let me ask you where are you going with this?"

10. To make sure you've answered the question, simply ask, when you've finished answering, "Did that answer your question?" If not continue with the discussion.

11. Suppose someone says that you have answered the question, but you can surmise by their expression or attitude that you haven't.

These are people who don't like to be intrusive or pushy. You need to acknowledge that by saying, in effect, "I get the impression that I haven't really answered all of that question. What part of it do we need to cover better?"

12. Suppose you ask for questions and there aren't any. You can move on or you can say, if there usually are questions on that topic, "Some people in our previous seminars have had a question about (whatever). Who would like to know a little more about that?"

13. On the other hand, when you ask for questions, it is not unusual for several hands to go up at once. It's important that you handle this skillfully. Here's how. Say that you will take questions in this order, and point to three random hands that are raised. I usually point to hands from three different parts of the room, which looks fairer than if they're all from one section. Then, take the questions in that order. If you forget the order, ask the audience; they will usually remember. Let the audience know you will get to as many of the others with raised hands afterwards. This procedure helps avoid participants constantly and frantically raising hands after each question is answered, trying to be recognized. If most of the questions are coming from one side of the room, you can light-heartedly tell the audience that those folks are doing all the work for everyone, and doesn't someone from the other side want to uphold the honor of that group.

14. If questions continue to come and you want to move on, you can say that we need to continue with the program now, and you will be sure to handle all questions by the time the seminar is over, so write down your question so you don't forget it.

15. If a questioner catches you in an apparent error or paradox, acknowledge it, thank them for clearing that up, and move on if they are right. If they are in error, explain why.

16. If you get a question about material that will be covered later in the program, say so, and you can add that that putting the ques-

tion in a fuller context will give a more meaningful answer. If you can give a short answer now, do so, and ask the audience to be sure to cover the question in detail when you come to that section of the seminar.

8

ROLE PLAYING

Role playing plays a key part in any dialogue that is two way and unscripted. Two leading disciplines that are best learned by role playing are those of selling and collecting bad debt. Since selling and collecting in-house trainings and public seminars are so commonly conducted all around the country and the world, every presenter is well served by learning to become a master of role playing, regardless of the seminar topic.

Learning to role play masterfully is not easy. For most people, it can take months or more. The reason is that, to be successful, you must get "out of your head" and into that of the other person, as I have said repeatedly. When I role play, I never worry what I am going to say. I know what my objectives are, and I don't think much about my response, although there are some classics that simply get you through the initial resistance but are of no help as the conversation proceeds. My focus is entirely on the other person; what they are saying and not saying, and how they feel. More on that later.

A comment about the similarities between selling and collecting: in both cases, there is a limited amount of time. The sales person cannot spend equal time on every prospect or client. Better prospects and great clients deserve more time. With sales prospects, the discipline is called "qualifying the prospect". The collector also cannot spend equal time with each unpaid account. Accounts that are larger and have more and better information justify spending more time on them. With debtors, the discipline is called "resolving the account." How either of these is done best will require an understanding of what is commonly called the "left brain" and the "right brain". I'll discuss that in the next chapter.

Whether resolving an account or qualifying a prospect, the professional collector or sales person is ultimately using their gut feelings, not unlike the professional gambler, who "knows" when to hold 'em and when to fold 'em. But, I don't want to make this sound weird, mysterious, or unfathomable, like the Ouiji Board of old. With practice, you can get very good at it. And, when you train *others* to role play, you will usually have gotten *very* good at it.

Let me be clear: The *single* best tool for learning either to sell or to collect is role playing. Scripts are for amateurs. They simply allow you to get *started* in a dialogue. Scripts are of no help, whatever, in the inevitable back-and-forth dialogue that follows the initial words.

So, why do people avoid role playing. Often, they feel, or they know, that they will do it "wrong", and it's embarrassing to make a public fool of yourself. Other observers say that role playing isn't "real" or it's not what they would encounter in a real dialogue. I can assure you that the other person's comments and your reactions in a role playing situation will feel real enough.

Doing role playing "wrong" is an essential step along the way to doing it well. A good analogy is how movies are made. Directors usually shoot as much as 100 times more film than is needed for the finished movie we eventually see on the screen. The actors do the takes over and over until the director is satisfied. What you don't see in the finished film are the outtakes that wind up on the cutting room floor. Role playing is your cutting room floor and is just as essential.

Here are the rules for role playing, again using sales or collecting seminars as the focus.

- *Only two people get to talk.* One person plays the debtor or sales prospect; the other person plays the collector or the sales person. Everyone else has to agree to be quiet, which often is not easy. Usually, things are said that cause laughter in the room. In other cases, people will be tempted to shout out responses or make editorial comments about what the players are saying. Discourage all of that ahead of time.

- *Each player must stay in the role.* Say whatever you want to say, but stay in the role. Do not allow phrases such as, "If I were in that situation, I'd say...." Or, "That happened to me once, and what I said was....". No war stories, please. Say what you want to say in *this* situation, because each situation and dialogue is *unique*. The words and feelings are never the same, even by the same two antagonists on two separate but identical sounding encounters.

- *The players should not look at each other.* There's less stress if they don't, even though in the real world, sales calls are often made face to face, as well as by phone.

- *Non-playing members of the group must actively listen.* The reason is that they will be asked to comment, when that role playing exercise is finished, whether real communicating was going on or were scripts or "comebacks" simply being mouthed and not really connecting with the other person.

In a variation of one-on-one role playing, an entire group can participate. Form a circle of chairs. Two people begin the exercise. Eventually, one or the other will run out of things to say, at which point someone else in the group jumps in. Almost always, someone will be available to pick up the conversational slack because the non-playing members of the group aren't under the pressure that is usually felt by the original two players. They are freer to listen to what's really going on. Another variation is having the group pair up, two by two. It gets noisy when everyone is talking at the same time, but everyone gets to experience the encounters more frequently. With this method, the trainer needs to walk around the room to observe and make comments, as needed.

Once again, the ultimate goal of role playing is to get to the point that you are so focused on what's going on with the other person that it's unnecessary to devote much energy to what you're thinking. *You are actively listening.* I realize that these words may not mean much because they describe an experience. It's like trying to describe a sneeze. No verbal description compares to actually sneezing, yourself. When you sneeze, only then do you really know what a sneeze is all about.

- *How to begin.* Since I'm still focused on selling and collecting, I'll use examples from these two activities. With collections, which is almost always done on the phone, either the debtor or the collector can begin talking. The collector may know what the situation is all about or may know nothing. Debtor excuses to work with can include, for example, "The manager is a friend", "I never got the bill", "My spouse handles all the bills", "I'll pay you when I get paid", "Your product was no good", "The check is in the mail", "I'm out of work", and so on.

  With a sales situation, the excuses may include, "I'm happy with my current vendor", "Your prices are too high", "I've been working with Jim at Shelby Company. He's my brother-in-law", "I don't make that decision", "We really don't need any", "I'm too busy to talk now", and so on.

- *Wrap up.* When each role play exercise is finished, the trainer guides the participants through a series of four followup questions.

  1. *How did you feel going through that?* More often than not, the answer will be what they *would have* felt, not what they actually *did* feel at the time. Often, the feeling is anger, discomfort, embarrassment, or other so-called negative feelings. I find that the role player is often reluctant to put himself or herself, as well as the other party, through that emotional experience (assuming the role player admits to having had one). The participants also commonly say that they didn't feel anything. Instead, they talk about the situation in every way but how they felt. When that happens, I press continuously with the ques-

tion, "Yes, but how did that feel?" If they still resist stating that they felt anything, I'll ask, "Did you enjoy that?" The answer is usually, "No.", which helps to point out that they did, in fact, feel *something*.

One purpose of role playing, then is to legitimize whatever feelings are being experienced. The feelings are neither right or wrong, nor is it the collector's or sales person's job to shield the debtor or sales prospect from their discomfort. Above all, it is crucial that participants realize that feelings are a key, if not *the* key, component of a dialogue.

2. *Ask the group what techniques were used, which could have been used, what seemed to work, what didn't, and why.* These questions let everyone become more aware of all that is happening in a fast moving verbal encounter. This exercise helps participants become more aware of what they were conscious of and what they were not. The question almost always produces a vigorous discussion of comments, which the trainer will either confirm, correct, or lead a discussion about them.

3. *Ask the debtor (or sales prospect) if the collector (or sales person) was in communication with the debtor (or prospect) or were they just mouthing desperate replies.* They can usually explain whether there was a real connection or did it feel like "two ships passing in the night". *Also ask the group.* My experience is that most of the group won't know, even though they were there the whole time! Being in communication is difficult—both to do and to observe—because doing so requires a high level of acknowledgement of the other person's communication and an awareness of what they are really thinking and feeling. The trainer should be able to point out where the communication broke down.

4. *Finally, ask the group what they think is the likelihood that the debtor will pay or the sales prospect will buy, on a scale of 1 to 10, where 1 is hopeless and 10 is money in the bank.* Experience has

shown that most observers, when the role playing exercise is completed, will have a good sense of the probability of success or failure or the degree in-between, even though they may not have been aware of how well the communication was done in the interim. Therefore, the better the job of role playing is done, the more accurate will be the qualifying of the sales prospect or the resolving of the debtor's account.

- Be prepared for skeptics who ask, "What if the debtor or prospect had said this, that, or whatever?" The answer is that you can respond only to what *is* said, not to what is *not* said. Anyway, and this is crucial, <u>both sides make it all up</u>, or they should, if they are willing to get away from scripts and "comebacks' and deal only with what is going on second by second. This is, admittedly, not easy, and it will take time, but the payoff is money in the bank as well as an incredible sense of achievement.

- If you do role playing exercises systematically and skillfully, I have found that you can expect at least a 20% improvement in productivity! But, watch out for resistance—it can wear you out. On the other hand, even though most people are reluctant to volunteer for role playing, once they get started, it can be awfully hard to get them to stop. It becomes fun!

- In any role playing exercise, when the leader senses that the conversation is going nowhere, which happens most of the time, eventually, it's appropriate to stop it.

- Incidentally, role playing often is valuable for uncovering more clearly where your sales program or payment policies need to be clarified or changed. This has been a huge, unexpected benefit for more than a few companies.

9

THE BRAIN AND RESISTANCE

In this chapter, we go deeply into what some would call psychological matters. In examining the left and the right "sides" of the brain, we are looking basically at logical as compared to emotional ways of reacting and communicating. It's incredibly valuable to understand the distinction between the two, because, as many people have noted, over the years, logic gets you only so far. If you've ever tried to reason with someone who is absolutely set in their ways and convinced of the correctness of their position, you know what I mean.

Even so, that doesn't mean that you ought not be logical or rational. Far from it. We need rational, scientific thinking in order to carry out so many of our jobs and even for survival. For example, we want pilots to be very analytical in how they fly the plane. We don't want them to feel a surge of creativity and do some loop-de-loops, at least not while we're passengers. Mathematical formulas should mean the same no matter how they are used. The examples are endless.

But, and this is a major but, it doesn't take much, when we are communicating, for the emotions to take over. We are all human, and we have a full range of emotional responses, including anger, sulking, screaming, feelings of pleasure, resentment, love, wishing, stunned silence, eagerness, sadness, and more.

And, if we consider the previous list of examples as "normal" feelings, we need to add the extreme feelings of people that are characterized as psychotic, bi-polar, suffering from post traumatic stress disorder, dementia, and a whole host of other abnormalities.

Now, let's look at a more detailed analysis of the left brain and the right brain. Then we will examine how an understanding of the differences can be so valuable in knowing how best to respond to logical vs. emotional communications, and how to know which you are confronting, so that you can make the most of the dialogue. You won't win them all, but you will definitely increase the odds of understanding where you are in the dialogue.

The left brain is usually considered to handle from 40% to 60% of our communications and learning. The remaining 60% to 40% is managed by the right brain.

Here are some common attributes of the left brain:

Rational   Logical   Analytical   Deals in Black and White

Certain   Intellectual   Parental   Nerdy   Knowing   Verbal

Understanding   Controlling   Convincing   Thinking   "Strong"

Categories of people that tend to use a heavy dose of their left brain include accountants, lawyers, pilots, mathematicians, doctors, and engineers.

Now for the typical attributes of the right brain:

Emotional   Gut Feelings   Creative   Experiential   Shades of Grey

Ambiguity   Intuitiveness   Childish   Social   "Getting It"

Persuade/Empower   Fantasize/Daydream Sensing   Being

"Weak"   Visual   Artistic

Finally, and at the risk of sounding presumptuous, I believe that our educational system, and especially the teachers who populate it, would greatly benefit by a better understanding and the systematic use of the psychology and the techniques for handling resistance in the classroom. The teachers would become more valuable (read: higher pay potential), and the students could only gain from moving through their sometimes open and often passive resistance to learning. And, obviously, the country benefits in so many ways from a better educated citizenry.

My reading of the educational landscape tells me that there are a number of predictable barriers to learning that students set up, and not always consciously. Examples include:

- "Sports are my thing. What do I need to learn this crap for?"
- "I'm bored."
- 'I better not let them know how smart I am."
- "I can always look this up on Google."
- "I'm gonna' be a dentist. What do I care about history?"
- "When is recess?"

You get the idea. But, how we get these insights incorporated into the educational system is beyond my ability to implement. Still, I can dream.

Categories of people who typically rely heavily on their right brains include artists, therapists, designers, actors, and all sorts of subtle and creative people.

In the real world, of course, people use both sides of their brains. It just depends on the situation which side is more heavily involved. Having stated the obvious, we need to look at how this understanding of the brain allows us to maximize our skill in presenting seminars, doing selling or collecting.

One of the key skills in conducting a seminar is the ability to handle resistance. Resistance may be expressed as outright spoken disagreement, shaking of the head, or else by a silence and an attitude that leads to the same conclusion. The pro will acknowledge the resistance or else no progress will be made. At the senior management level of companies, those that insist on doing things the same old way, because "that's how we've always done it", often get left behind as the business environment changes, which is constantly does. That type of resistance is a company killer.

One way to acknowledge the resistance is to say, "You're not buying that, are you?" or any words to that effect. You can add, "Let's talk about this some more." If you are selling, and the prospect says something like, "I'm happy with my present supplier", one classic response, which legitimizes that sentiment but still may open the door to have the prospect consider you is to say, "I admire you and your supplier for developing such a good relationship." Then, to probe for possible openings, you can add, "If there was one thing you wished they could do better, what would that be?" There usually is *something*, and you can explore and exploit that opening. I grant you that the initial response is scripted, but, after that, you are on your own.

Another probing comment might be, "*Our* clients really love us, and here's why." Then talk about elements of your product or service that might be better than that of the other supplier and could open the door to your prospect wanting to hear more. Again, the ongoing dialogue will be completely unscripted.

With telephone bill collectors, debtors often get upset and may shout or curse. Since logical comments about the obligation to pay the bill are likely to be a waste of time, the best approach is to acknowledge the upset. You might say, "I'm really sorry if I've upset you" (although, technically, you don't upset people, they create the upset themselves), and continue talking about how upsetting this must be. You might even be able to add that you don't want to be one of those people who are adding to their problems.

Instead, you want to help them. They might want to hear how you can help.

Basically, acknowledging the resistance greatly improves the probability of your eliminating it. Here are some examples of what I call "bridging statements" that increase your odds of moving past the resistance so that the other person can be more open to hear your point of view:

- That's an excellent question.
- I don't blame you for saying that.
- I know pretty much how you feel.
- I wish we could do it that way.
- Many people have said that.
- It certainly seems that way.
- Yes, that's true.
- Obviously, you have a good reason why you feel that way.

The last bridge is especially useful for someone who just feels the way they do. It has the tendency—no guarantees—to allow that person to take a look at what the reasons might be, which you can then deal with, or to acknowledge that they really have no reason at all, so they can move past the blind resistance. On the other hand, their response might be, "No, I don't have any reason whatsoever. I just feel that way." You can't win them all!

The bridges are an essential middle step between the question or objection and the response. They help assure the other person that you understand, appreciate, and "get" where they're coming from and how they feel about that. That tends to neutralize the ability of their feelings to block their left brain from rationally hearing what you want to say. Only after you have made a bridging statement do you then begin your reply and whatever dialogue follows.

Some observers have said that bridging statements are manipulative. I concur that manipulation is going on, but it isn't you who is doing it. Bridges are a way to keep others from manipulating *you* with their out-of-control emotions.

In the seminar room, you want to be continuously looking around at all of the participants to see how they are reacting, or not reacting, to what is going on. Check with them frequently, either individually or with the entire group, by asking questions such as, **"Are you with me on this?"**, **or, "Does that make sense?", or, "Am I going too fast?" or, "Does this interest you?" or, "Who has an example of that?" or, "What do you think?",** etc., etc. Vary these questions. Asking the same one repeatedly becomes tiring for much of the audience.

Basically, there is no excuse for creating a boring seminar if the presenter knows how to stay in touch with the audience, get plenty of feedback, acknowledge and seek out questions and feelings, and avoid doing the things described in chapter two, the typical bad seminar.

The presenter knows what he or she wants to cover and accomplish. The actual material covered and the back-and-forth dialogue with the attendees will be different with *every* audience, for the obvious reason that each audience is different. Yet, the resulting audience comments can be equally outstanding when the presenter does the job using all the tools I have described. This is what it means when I stated earlier that you need to get out of your head and into those of your audience. The "high" you can achieve after *every* such presentation is very satisfying, indeed.

10

ENDING THE PRESENTATION

As you approach the end of the program, there are a number of consider-ations to cover. Here are the key ones.

- **End on time**—Make it your business to keep an eye on the watch that is on the podium. Participants will expect you not only to start on time but also to end pretty much on time. However, if you end a few minutes early or go over by a few minutes, that's no problem. If you have some good material to cover and you need to go well past the stated ending time to cover it, ask the audience if that's OK. They will usually agree enthusiastically, because they want to get what they came for.

- **Some closing comments**—Obviously, you will thank everyone for attending. Observe that you want to be sure that everyone got what they came for and, if not, be sure to let you know. If there is a host-ing organization, they receive your thanks, as well.

- **Get an evaluation from everyone**—The best way to do this is to have the audience fill out just the identifying information—name, address, phone number, company name, title, etc.—earlier in the program, such as after the last break. This makes the whole process less of a bother at the end. Then, before making your closing com-ments, ask the audience to complete the remainder of the form, which asks for information about the quality of the program and the presenter, what should have been included or omitted, what do they plan to do as a result of the program, and would they like to be contacted about the product or service you may be offering.

- **<u>Provide an incentive to get all the evaluations</u>**—At minimum, ask people to pass the evaluations to the end of each aisle, where an associate will pick them up. An even better approach is to have an incentive, such as a completion certificate, that you will hand out as each participant brings the completed evaluation form up to you at the end of the program. Incidentally, when you ask everyone to complete their evaluations, there will be a minute or two of silence while people are writing, at the conclusion of which you ask, "How many have finished the evaluation?" Not everyone will have done so, so you say that we'll take a few minutes more. Notice that I am going into great detail about getting all the evaluations completed and collected; that's how important I consider them, in terms of helping assure the best, most consistent quality you can produce.

- **<u>Stay to talk</u>**—One of your concluding comments should be your willingness to stay for a while to talk further with anyone who wishes to discuss anything covered in the program. You may receive business cards to follow up on, or you may be asked for your business card. Have several available. If you have a book to offer and anyone buys it at the end of the meeting, offer to sign it. For people who buy my book, "The Check Is NOT In The Mail," I write a personal comment, add, "My best to you" and sign my name.

11

MISCELLANEOUS

Now, I want to discuss a number of important issues that, individually, do not take a full chapter to cover.

What to charge—Some seminars are free. You just want to get the bodies in the room. Other seminars are intended to make money. To maximize the profit, you need to do split-list testing, particularly if you are mailing brochures or any kind of mailing piece.

Split-list testing means dividing the alphabet roughly in half, which is usually A through L and M through Z. Each half gets a different attendance fee, and you'll see which fee optimizes the return. At the seminar, itself, you can offer to refund the difference to those who paid the higher fee, and you will explain that this was an experiment. For public seminars, offer a reduced price for any organization that enrolls two or more or three or more.

Program length—Some programs, such as at a Rotary Club meeting, may be limited to 20 minutes. Typical seminars are usually not less than two hours in length. Depending on the material to be covered, you could have a three hour program, either in the morning or in the afternoon, or you may need to spend six hours, which is commonly from 9 A. M. to noon, then 1 P. M. to 4 P.M.

Credits—Many professional organizations require their members to take a certain number of hours of continuing education meetings each year, in order to retain their professional status and licenses. Included among these groups are doctors, pharmacists, realtors and attorneys. You will need to get your program accredited by these accrediting organizations, and you will definitely include that information on the invitational material. At the completion of your seminar, have the authorizing documents available from the accrediting organization, fill out and sign the sections that pertain to you, and give to the attendees.

For those programs not geared to audiences that require professional certification, I have found it useful to create an official looking Certificate of Completion for the program just ended. Many participants value such certificates and proudly hang them on the wall at work.

Promotion—If you have the benefit of a sponsoring organization, give them plenty of relevant information about your qualifications and experience in the topic to be covered. This gives them what they need to promote the program most successfully. Even if it's an in-house company meeting, and attendance is not required, the same kind of information helps increase the attendance.

For public seminars, where it's up to you to get the people in the room, you need a variety of proven methods to maximize attendance. If you're doing mass mailings, two mailings are often more cost effective than just one. The question is WHEN to do the mailings. Because people usually plan and fill their calendars well ahead, the first mailing should go out about five to six weeks in advance, with the second mailing at two to three weeks ahead.

The returns from mass mailings usually are no greater than 1% to 3%, but that is often enough to make for a profitable seminar. The second mailing may just break even when you compare the cost of the mailing vs. the income it produces. Still, the extra bodies in the room can have value in future sales of products or services.

You will want to do a lot of testing. As I discussed earlier in this chapter on split-list testing, you will want to test different brochure designs, lunch or no lunch, length of the seminar, copy used, special offers, if any, as well as cost of the seminar. And, unless the mailing goes to just one type of industry, you will want to test different SIC codes. These are the designations by which various types of industries are categorized. Your mailing house can assist you in getting this information.

You also want to make it easy for potential attendees to buy. In addition to cash and checks, get in touch with VISA and MasterCard, so that you can take payment in the form that many businesses and individuals prefer.

Test black and white flyers vs. color. Test an 8 ½ by 11 inch paper compared to a larger, typically 11 by 17 inch, folded brochure.

One more idea: invite your current clients to come to the seminar. You can let them attend at no cost and with the idea that they will pick up more that they may not have absorbed the first time. The benefits of this approach are two-fold. First, you help solidify your relationship with your client and can also increase the chance of getting referrals. Second, with satisfied clients in the seminar room, they can be a valuable source of positive comments from satisfied users, which may be all it takes to push some on-the-fence attendees to want your product or service.

Selling products or services—Except for military briefings, religious gatherings, sessions in the classroom, and the like, you may want to sell a product or service. Do not make it difficult to buy, either at the seminar or afterward. If you are offering a service, give people ways to either sign up at the seminar or at least fill out a form that asks you to contact them later. At the very least, for those who do not ask you to contact them, you will call on them after the seminar. What have you got to lose? The worst they can do is say no. Those are good odds.

But even if they say no, the professional always asks for references—"Who do you know who is not in as good shape as you are and could use our help?" Again, you have nothing to lose, and you sometimes do get a reference.

Training others—If you become so successful in presenting programs that you can no longer do them all, you may need others to do some of the presentations, but you want to be sure that each of them is as good as you are. You will know that by reading the evaluation forms. So, how do you get others up to speed? Start with people who have the essential knowledge about the subject and want to be involved as a presenter. Finding knowledgeable people may be the easier part. The more difficult job is training them to be effective presenters.

To help train your associates more quickly, they need to practice in front of you and, if available, other people, to comprise an audience. You will definitely want to include plenty of role-playing exercises that they must conduct, until they become un-self-conscious about it. Ideally, you should video tape them and play the results back to them. Then, they can see how they appear, whether or not they are moving around too much or doing other distracting body movements, how well they speak, handle questions, manage the time, or anything else that either enhances the overall experience or detracts from it.

Getting experience—In addition to the training described above, and particularly if you are just starting out, yourself, it helps to get some experience with venues that are safe, such as with a group of friends or family, and with audiences where it really doesn't matter if you are not the best you can be yet, such as with Rotary Club meetings or local Chamber of Commerce sessions. If you have friends in the audience, ask them how you did and how you could do better. It's also a good idea to join Toastmasters, particularly if you are very knowledgeable in your subject but inexperienced or even terrified about speaking in front of others.

12

SUMMING UP

- The people who tend to get the most out of a seminar are from those organizations from which both a manager and staff personnel attend together. The reason is that they will have shared a common experience and had an opportunity to both learn and move through at least some of the resistance to a new idea, although each individual obviously handles the learning and the resistance somewhat differently. Still, it was a shared experience, and that counts for a lot, as we'll see when we look at the alternatives, below.

The next best likelihood of positive change coming from the seminar is that in which the manager is there, but without staff. Managers are in a position to order changes, and staff is expected to carry out the management directives, although some "selling" and explaining may be needed to get full acceptance.

The worst results, relatively speaking, can be found in those organizations from which staff only attended. I have too often heard, at the end of a seminar, "Now, we have to go back and sell the great stone face on this." In other words, since the manager wasn't there to have the experience that the staff had, the staff has to do the selling and hope the manager gets through whatever resistance to change exists. In the real world, managers will buy a concept more easily from the expert in front of the room, rather than from those people he or she manages.

Unfortunitely, the great majority of public seminar audiences are staff only. The boss may have sent them as a nice "perk" or with the advice to "go learn about this, and come back and tell me all about it." Still, staff only is better than no one attending at all.

- The main goal of your presentation is to communicate as much of your expertise as possible. Hold nothing back. Not only does it feel great to be the expert in front of an audience and know that you have served them well, but an outstanding seminar allows you to gain new business on a wholesale basis.

- I have found that the more seminars you do, the more you will learn. I tell every group I speak to that although they are learning from me, I am also learning from them, which is literally true, simply because each attendee has information and experiences that I don't, and the collective input from all these people only solidifies the 'real world" relevance of what you are saying. If nothing else, your audiences will teach you how to continuously improve and make more pertinent each successive program.

- Finally, I have enjoyed sharing, through this book, my years of marketing, presenting, and training others to do the best seminars possible. I would be happy to further assist you and answer questions you may have. You can e-mail me at lenwriter@aol.com. A simple question will get a response in a day or two—no charge. For more extensive consulting, I'll charge you, and you get to pay in advance! That's my collection experience kicking in. What did you expect?

www.ingramcontent.com/pod-product-compliance
Lightning Source LLC
Chambersburg PA
CBHW021048180526
45163CB00005B/2330